THE BIG BOOK OF ICELAND FACTS

AN EDUCATIONAL COUNTRY TRAVEL PICTURE BOOK FOR KIDS ABOUT HISTORY, DESTINATION PLACES, ANIMALS AND MANY MORE

Iceland is a country located in Europe, in the North Atlantic Ocean. Iceland is a great place to experience nature and outdoor activities, from hiking and camping to skiing and snowboarding.

The capital city of Iceland is Reykjavik, which is also the country's largest city.

Iceland is known as the "Land of Fire and Ice" because it has volcanoes and glaciers.

The population of Iceland is about 364,000 people.

The official language of Iceland is Icelandic.

Iceland is the least densely populated country in Europe.

Iceland was settled by Vikings in the 9th century.

Iceland is known for its stunning natural beauty, including waterfalls, geysers, and hot springs.

Iceland is home to the famous Blue Lagoon, a geothermal spa where people can relax in warm, mineral-rich water.

Iceland's national animal is the gyrfalcon, a type of bird of prey.

The Icelandic krona is the currency used in Iceland.

Iceland is known for its delicious seafood, including fish and lobster.

Iceland is one of the few countries in the world that still has an active whaling industry.

Icelanders believe in elves and trolls, and there are many stories and legends about these mythical creatures.

Iceland has a unique landscape, with black sand beaches, lava fields, and glaciers.

Iceland is home to the largest glacier in Europe, called Vatnajökull.

The Icelandic flag is blue with a red cross, and it features a white cross inside the red one.

Iceland has a high standard of living, and it is ranked as one of the happiest countries in the world.

Iceland is a very safe country, with a low crime rate.

The Icelandic alphabet has 32 letters, including some that are unique to the language.

Iceland is a popular filming location for movies and TV shows, including Game of Thrones and Star Wars.

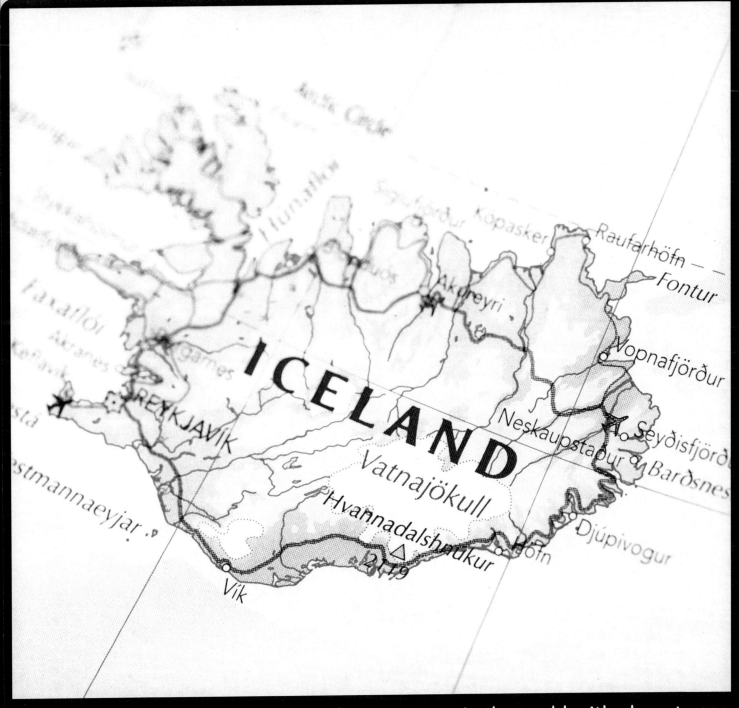

Iceland has one of the highest literacy rates in the world, with almost 100% of the population able to read and write.

Iceland has a strong tradition of storytelling, and there are many books and sagas written in Icelandic.

Iceland is a member of NATO and the United Nations.

Iceland has a women's football team that is ranked among the top in the world.

Iceland is home to many hot springs and geysers, including the famous Geysir.

Icelanders have a strong connection to their Viking heritage, and they often celebrate Viking culture with festivals and reenactments.

Iceland is located near the Arctic Circle, which means that during the summer months, the sun never fully sets.
Iceland has a unique cuisine that includes dishes like fermented shark and smoked lamb.

Iceland is a popular destination for tourists who want to see the Northern Lights.
Iceland has a strong tradition of knitting, and Icelandic wool is famous for its warmth and durability.

Iceland is one of the most environmentally friendly countries in the world, with almost all of its electricity coming from renewable sources.

Iceland has a high life expectancy, with the average person living to be over 80 years old.
Iceland has a small film industry, but it has produced some award-winning movies, including "Rams" and "The County."

Iceland has a rich musical tradition, and many famous musicians have come from Iceland, including Bjork and Of Monsters and Men. Iceland is home to the largest puffin population in the world.

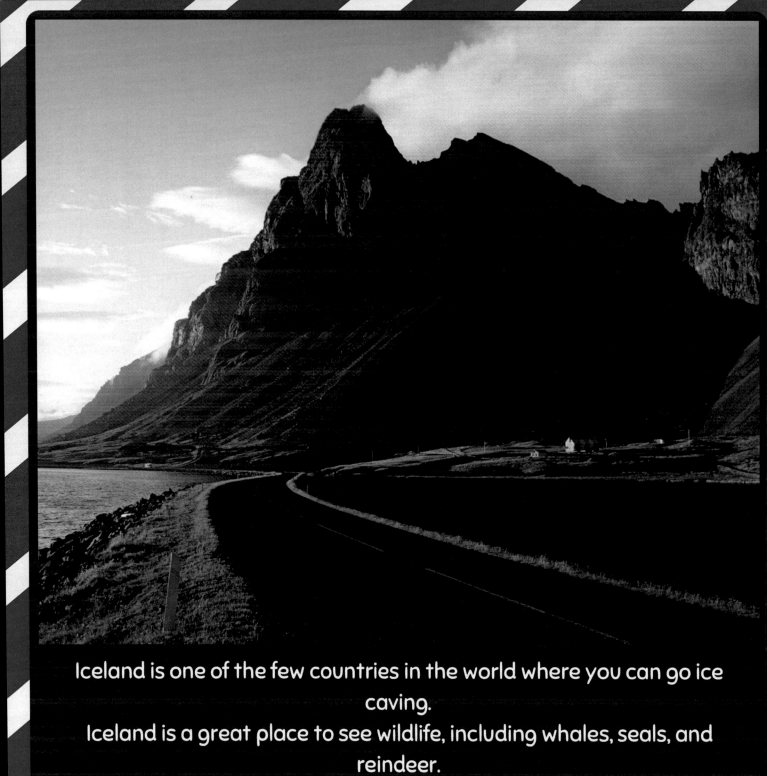

Iceland is one of the few countries in the world where you can go ice caving.
Iceland is a great place to see wildlife, including whales, seals, and reindeer.

Iceland is a very eco-friendly country, and many people ride bikes or walk instead of driving.
Iceland is known for its beautiful waterfalls, including the famous Gullfoss waterfall.

Iceland is home to one of the largest geothermal power plants in the world.
Iceland is a great place to see geology in action, with frequent volcanic eruptions and earthquakes.

Icelanders have a strong tradition of swimming, and many towns have public swimming pools that are open year-round.

Iceland has a unique Christmas tradition, where people give each other books as gifts on Christmas Eve.
Iceland has a small but thriving film industry, and many international productions are filmed there.

BEST PLACES TO VISIT IN ICELAND:

- Reykjavik – The capital city of Iceland, known for its colorful buildings and lively nightlife.
- Blue Lagoon – A geothermal spa located in a lava field, famous for its warm, mineral-rich water.
- Golden Circle – A popular tourist route that includes Thingvellir National Park, Geysir, and Gullfoss waterfall.
- Vatnajökull National Park – Home to Vatnajökull, the largest glacier in Europe, as well as stunning ice caves and other natural wonders.
- Jökulsárlón – A glacier lagoon filled with icebergs that have broken off from the nearby glacier.
- Skaftafell – A national park located beneath Vatnajökull glacier, with hiking trails and stunning views.
- Akureyri – The largest town outside of the Reykjavik area, known for its vibrant cultural scene and beautiful scenery.
- Westfjords – A remote and rugged region of Iceland known for its stunning fjords and wildlife.
- Myvatn – A region of Iceland known for its volcanic landscapes, hot springs, and birdlife.
- Snæfellsnes Peninsula – A scenic region of Iceland known for its diverse landscapes, including mountains, glaciers, and lava fields.
- Húsavík – A small town in northern Iceland known for its whale watching tours.
- Landmannalaugar – A region of Iceland known for its colorful mountains and hot springs.
- Thorsmork – A valley located between three glaciers, known for its stunning scenery and hiking trails.
- Dynjandi – A waterfall located in the Westfjords region, known for its beauty and tranquility.
- Skogafoss – A waterfall located on the south coast of Iceland, known for its impressive height and power.

Travel Tips for Iceland:

- Dress in layers, as the weather in Iceland can be unpredictable.
- Pack waterproof and windproof clothing, as well as sturdy hiking shoes.
- Rent a 4x4 vehicle if you plan on exploring Iceland's more remote regions.
- Make sure to bring plenty of cash, as some places in Iceland do not accept credit cards.
- Consider booking a guided tour to make the most of your time in Iceland.
- Take advantage of Iceland's natural hot springs, but be sure to follow local customs and etiquette.
- Be prepared for long daylight hours in the summer and long periods of darkness in the winter.
- Book accommodations and rental cars well in advance, as Iceland is a popular tourist destination.
- Respect Iceland's delicate natural environment by staying on designated paths and not littering.
- Try local Icelandic cuisine, including fish, lamb, and skyr (a type of yogurt).
- Be prepared for high prices in Iceland, as it is one of the most expensive countries in the world.
- Check the weather forecast before heading out, as the weather in Iceland can change quickly.
- Bring a good camera to capture Iceland's stunning landscapes and wildlife.
- Be aware of the potential hazards of driving in Iceland, including gravel roads and narrow bridges.
- Respect Iceland's wildlife and do not disturb or feed any animals.

Made in United States
North Haven, CT
12 December 2024

62377490R00024